Hazel Bean learns to take turns

Author Sarah Walsh
Illustrated by Gemma Tetley
This book is dedicated to my Goddaughter Hazel.

Share & Be Kind ♡
Sarah Walsh

Look out for Buddy the Bear.

How many times do you see him in the story?

This is Hazel Bean.

Hazel goes to Little Bears Pre-school and loves to play.

This is Hazel's friend Luke.

Luke wants to play with the Pirate ship too but when Hazel says, "No, it's mine," he doesn't know what to do.

Mrs McGreavey is listening and says, "I understand why you feel sad, Luke." She hugs him and suggests,

"Let's help Owen build his train track now, then you can have a turn with the Pirate ship and treasure chests."

Mrs McGreavey then asks, "Hazel, why is Luke feeling sad?"

Hazel replies, "He wants the Pirate ship but it's mine. He made me mad!"

...it is kind to take turns...

...with the other girls and boys."

"I have an idea,"

says Mrs McGreavey.

"Shall we ask Luke if he would like
to help you build a Treasure Island?"

"You can use the sand timer to take turns steering the Pirate ship around the Island," suggests Mrs McGreavey.

"Then maybe take turns using the telescope to look for treasure hidden in the sand."

Hazel shouts with excitement,

"Luke!!!"

"Do you want to make a Treasure Island with lots of shiny gold to find?"

Luke's face lights up. "Yes please," he says as he leaves the trains behind.

They work together, finding objects to make their spectacular shiny Treasure Island.

"Arrrgh!" says Hazel as she waves her sword.

Pirate Hazel sails the ship around the Island, then...

...remembering what Mrs McGreavey had said, she turns the sand timer over and lets Luke have a turn.

"Land ahoy!" shouts Luke.

"Let's get the sparkly treasure!" says Hazel.

They find the big **X** and then they dig...

...and **dig**...

...and **dig! Oops!**

They give each other a big Pirate High Five and say,

"Arrrgh!!!"

Mrs McGreavey is so proud of Hazel.

She gives her a gold star sticker and says,

REWARD CHART

BE KIND

SHARE

LISTEN

MON TUE

"It's so much fun...

...when you learn to take turns".

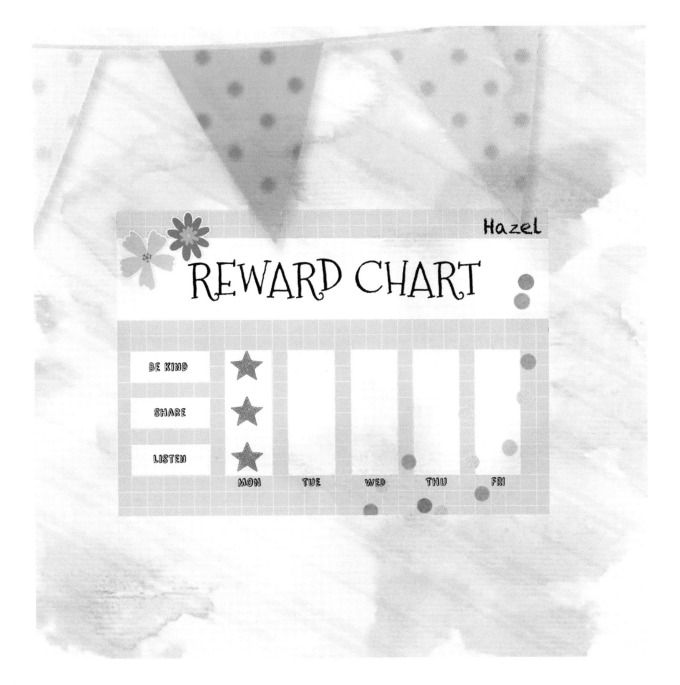

Did you spot Buddy <u>4</u> times?

Early Years Educators/Parents guide

Children who hear or read this story can be encouraged to think about their own actions and behaviours and how this affects the feelings of others.

This story also provides ideas to adults, who support children's learning, because the following effective approaches to supporting positive behaviour are used by the Early Years Educator in the story:

Distraction approach: Encouraging Luke to play with Owen distracted him and helped him learn how to tolerate delay when his needs were not met straightaway. Using the 'now' and 'then' strategy reassured Luke that he would have a turn soon. This also may have de-escalated any feelings of frustration or even aggressive behaviour that the situation might have caused.

Modelling positive culture: Mrs McGreavey demonstrated a caring and respectful attitude which encouraged Hazel to take turns. Hazel remembers, later on in the story, what Mrs McGreavey had suggested then chooses to be kind involving her friend in a playful scenario.

Praising and rewarding: Hazel was praised and rewarded a sticker for her kind behaviour and attitude, this may help to encourage the same positive behaviour again because she enjoyed this good experience.